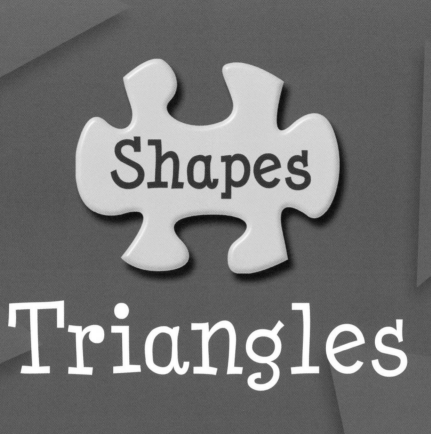

Shapes
Triangles

by Sarah L. Schuette

Reading Consultant:
Elena Bodrova, Ph.D., Senior Consultant
Mid-continent Research for Education and Learning

an imprint of Capstone Press
Mankato, Minnesota

A+ Books are published by Capstone Press
P.O. Box 669, 151 Good Counsel Drive, Mankato, Minnesota 56002
http://www.capstone-press.com

1 2 3 4 5 6 07 06 05 04 03 02

Library of Congress Cataloging-in-Publication Data
Schuette, Sarah L., 1976–
    Triangles / by Sarah L. Schuette.
    p.cm—(Shapes)
    Summary: Simple text, photographs, and illustrations show triangles in everyday objects.
    Includes bibliographical references and index.
    ISBN 0-7368-1465-5 (hardcover)
    I. Triangle—Juvenile literature. [1.Triangle.] Title.
QA482 .S385 2003
516'.15—dc21   2002000898

Created by the A+ Team

Sarah L. Schuette, editor; Heather Kindseth, art director and designer; Jason Knudson,
    designer and illustrator; Angi Gahler, illustrator; Gary Sundermeyer, photographer;
    Nancy White, photo stylist

Note to Parents, Teachers, and Librarians

The Shapes series uses color photographs and a nonfiction format to introduce children to the
shapes around them. It is designed to be read aloud to a pre-reader or to be read independently by
an early reader. The images help early readers and listeners understand the text and concepts
discussed. The book encourages further learning by including the following sections: Table of
Contents, Words to Know, Read More, Internet Sites, and Index. Early readers may need assistance
using these features.

Table of Contents

Triangles have three sides and are flat.

Triangles can even be food for a cat.

8

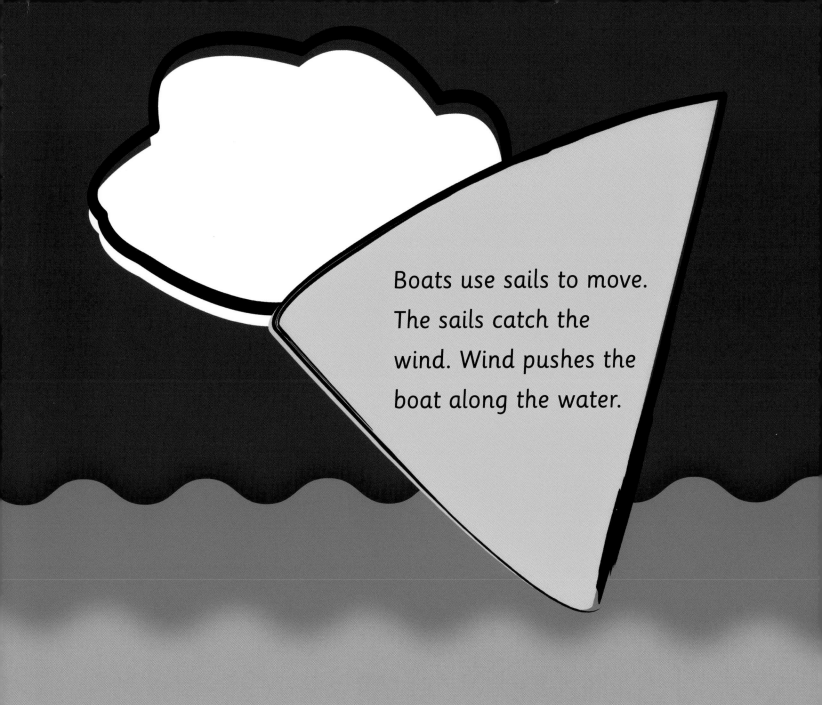

Boats use sails to move. The sails catch the wind. Wind pushes the boat along the water.

Sails are triangles on a boat.

9

Buttons keep shirts, coats, and other clothing closed. The buttons slide into buttonholes.

These triangles close up a coat.

11

A triangle patch
stays on with thread.

12

13

Go Te
Go
Cou

14

am

Team triangles are
blue and red.

ugars

15

16

Your body is made mostly of water just like a watermelon. Water helps to make watermelons juicy. You can eat every part of a watermelon, even the seeds and the rind.

Some triangles are juicy and sweet.

Pizza triangles
are fun to eat.

18

Bite these triangles and hear a crunch.

21

You can cut one square in half to make two triangles.

You might find triangles in your lunch.

23

Some signs have arrows. The arrows are triangles that tell people which way to go. Other signs are triangles that tell people to watch out.

Triangles point to the left and to the right.

24

25

Which triangle is shiny and bright?

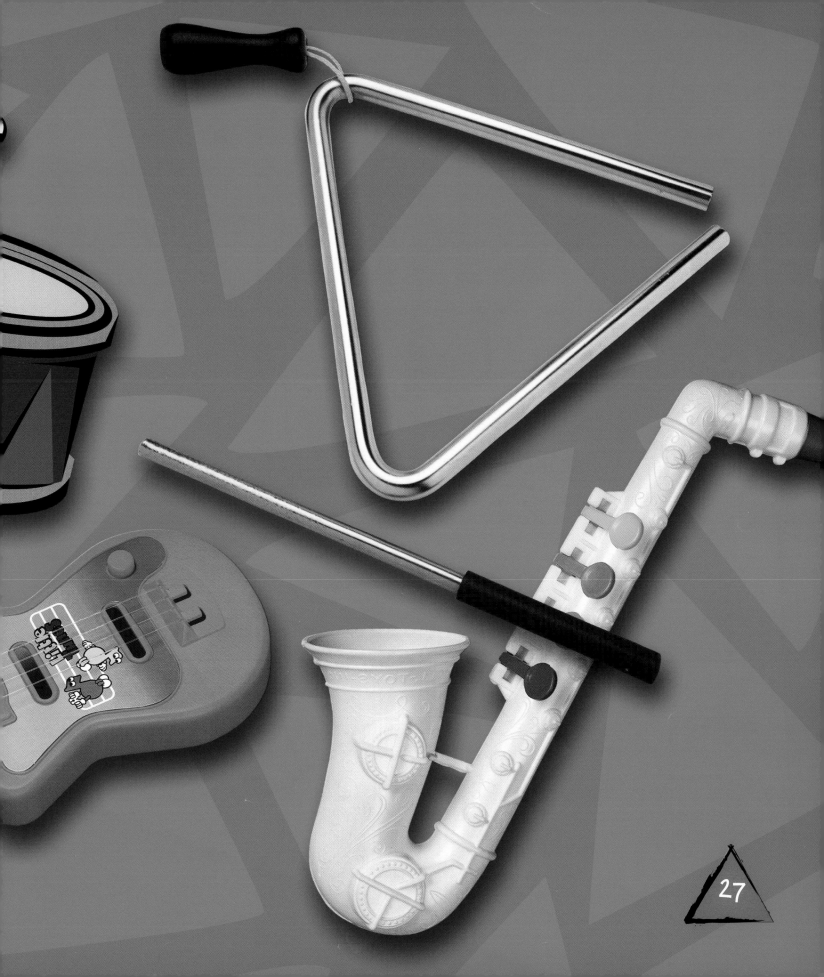

Play Triangle Toss

What you need

drinking straws

scissors

yarn

ruler

drinking cup

friends

28

1 Cut off the bottom of the straws below the bend. It takes three straw pieces to make one triangle.

2 Cut one 24-inch (60-centimeter) piece of yarn. Thread the yarn through all three pieces of straw. Tie together to make a triangle. Trim the ends of the yarn with a scissors. Repeat Steps 1 and 2 to make three triangles for each player.

3 Place the cup upside down in the middle of a room. Have your friends stand about 4 feet (1.2 meters) away from the cup.

4 Each player tries to toss a triangle so that it lands on or closest to the cup.

29

Words to Know

rind—the tough outer layer on melons, citrus fruits, and some cheeses; watermelon rinds are smooth and hard.

sail—a large sheet of strong cloth such as canvas that makes a boat move when it catches the wind; some sails are triangular in shape.

seed—the part of a flowering plant that can grow into a new plant; watermelons have black and white seeds.

thread—a strand of cotton or other material used for sewing; people sew patches on clothing to cover holes or stains.

Read More

Dotlich, Rebecca Kai. *What Is a Triangle?* Harper Growing Tree. New York: Harper Festival, 2000.

Onyefulu, Ifeoma. *A Triangle for Adaora: An African Book of Shapes.* New York: Dutton Children's Books, 2000.

Internet Sites

Track down many sites about triangles.
Visit the FACT HOUND at *http://www.facthound.com*

IT IS EASY! IT IS FUN!

1) Go to *http://www.facthound.com*
2) Type in: 0736814655
3) Click on "FETCH IT" and FACT HOUND will find several links hand-picked by our editors.

Relax and let our pal FACT HOUND do the research for you!

Index

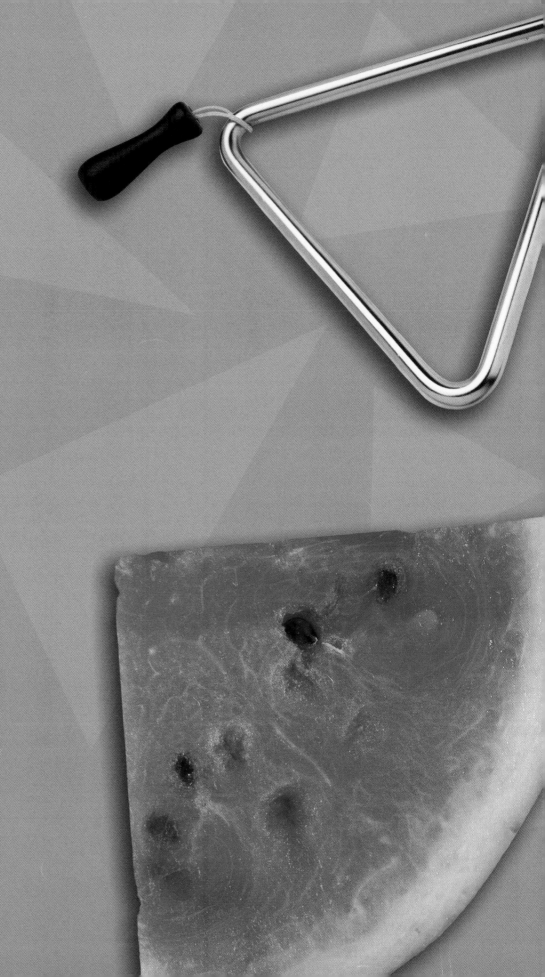